The Gift of
and other r

Norah,

    May the reflections in this book speak to what is deepest in you. With best wishes,

       Carmel Bracken.

The Gift of a Friend
and other verses

Carmel Bracken RSM

MERCIER PRESS

Mercier Press
PO Box 5, 5 French Church Street, Cork
24 Lower Abbey Street, Dublin 1

© Carmel Bracken 1992

ISBN 1 85635 031 2

To my family and friends
who have helped me find
'my voice'.

Printed in Ireland by Colour Books Ltd.

Contents

Introduction

Writing for me is a means of listening to the 'voices' of my heart – a way of being in touch with my deepest feelings, thoughts, dreams. Sometimes I feel that it is like opening Pandora's box. I have to listen to inner voices of loneliness, fear, anger, frustration before I can hear the quiet voices of hope, love, faith, God. The reflections in this book represent some of those different voices. They have been born out of my struggle to listen to God in the different voices of my heart, a listening that has deepened in me the awareness that God is not some Almighty Being that is beyond me but a Mystery within me. Perhaps these voices will echo your own.

This book is meant to be a kind of prayer book to help you as you journey within yourself to listen to your own voices.

At some stage within all our lives, we have to take responsibility for the person shaped by our past. We must accept and integrate that person into ourselves, building on what is helpful and allowing what is harmful to be healed. This means listening to our inner voices, allowing the truth and the person we are called to be, to be set free.

The Gift of a Friend

Countless people cross my path
Some pass and are gone
Their memory fading into oblivion
But there are ones who will never
Be forgotten
Their presence woven
Into the fabric of my life
Friends who touch my life's core
Who widen inner horizons
And cause new life
To spring up within
I thank God for those special friends
Who accept me as I am
And so free me to become.

Dancing Shoreline

The fear of being submerged
In icy waters
Momentarily held me back
From being one with you
But your dancing shoreline
Seduced me
Drawing me gradually
Into your depths
Your touch awakening
Dormant sensations
Waves of energy
Flowing freely
'Till my whole being
Was alive
To you.

Two Trees

Arms outstretched
You touch
One another
Foliage entwining
Becoming one

Yet there is
Space
In your togetherness
For life to flow
Between you
Two solitudes
Embracing
Yet not invading
The centre
Of the other.

Rugged Beauty

Its rugged beauty
Called forth
Something as yet
Unnamed
In me
And I longed
To sink deeper
And deeper
Into its earth
The need to be
One with its centre
Pulsing in my own.

Spiddal

Oh to have time
To remain
A while longer here
Where my life
Has no set
Agenda
Giving unrestricted scope
For something new
To emerge
In me
Where thoughts
That float
In vague suspension
Can crystallise
In a single moment.

Journey to the Sea

With ease you swoop
From your lofty perch
And fly to greet the sea

What sharp contrast
To my descent
With its unsure
Faltering steps

Yet the struggle
Was a necessary part
Of my journey
Wearing away defences
Until I was
Centred
By the soothing sound
Of the sea
Its strength seeping
Through my vulnerability
'Till its power could
Flow freely
Its fragrance refresh.

Essence

Warmth
Drawing from porous jar
Inner fragrance
Unassaulted essence
Disclosing its secret.

Stones

What do you feel
As you silently await
The incoming tide?
Do you fear that moment
Of being submerged
By a power greater
Than yourself
Or do you long
For its coming
The exhilarating feeling
As it flows about you
Leaving you fulfilled
And at peace
Knowing you are
What you were created
To be.

Space

You are struggling
I see it
Reflected in your eyes
And though
I ache
To hold you
'Till your pain
Subsides
I sense your need
For space
Space to find
Your answers
Or if not answers
The strength
To live with
The questions.

Challenge of the Tulips

They caught my eye
As I passed by
Tall and graceful that they were
Yet it was not their gracefulness
That held my gaze
But the beauty of their petals
Opening in response to the
Sun's caress
Their centres becoming visible
An openness which made them appear
So vulnerable
And left them exposed
To wind and rain
Yet they were so alive
Nothing held back
Their life lived with intensity
Reaching fullness
In the gentle surrendering
Of that life
Their openness disturbed me
As I stood confronted
By the weakness of my own response
To the outpouring of God's love.
Lead me Lord
Into that openness
So that I too
May be fully alive
And not just existing.

Dreamer

You had a dream
Powerful
Vibrant
Refusing to sleep
Or be restrained
By night-time fears
Leaping into daylight
In evocative dance
With reality.

And though your died
At the hands of those
Who feared your dream
Your dream lives on
And with it
You
Giving hope
To dreamers.

Revelation

So many words
Outpouring
Insisting on being written
Make me wonder
If they have been waiting
Inside
For me to give them outlet.

Interiority

Serenity
Of floodlit castle
Outlined against night sky
Held me motionless
'Till framed in space
I sank into quiet
No longer in flight

From interiority.

Waiting

As I wait here
Body feeling
But slight dis-ease
Not so out of tune
As to make me fear
Your pronouncement

I think of those
Who wait in fear
For you to confirm
What they already sense
Within
That they are losing
The battle
With an inner foe

I wonder if it were me
Would I be afraid to die
I guess I would
For sometimes
I'm afraid to live.

Harmony

Music
Deep
True
Drifting through the air
'Till it reached my room
Deepening my awareness
Of the God
Whose song
I want to sing
Resonating with
The harmony
That is His.

Sounds

Nature's sounds
Blending harmoniously
In tune
With the Creator
Not loud
Or harsh
But with a quiet integrity
That speaks more eloquently
Of God
Than any words
I could ever speak.

Eternity Moments

Moments
Charged with fullness
Eternity moments
Present permeating
Future
Moments
Diffusing barriers
Revealing beauty
Timelessness
Oneness.

Babbling Brook

As the light filters
Through the trees
And sparkles on you
The air echoes
With your music
'Till I'm left in
No doubt
As to who
Orchestrates.

Nests

The apparent simplicity
Of your nest
Built in peat moss bag
On closer look
Revealed much more
Intricate design
Utter perfection
Of love's preparation
For birthing.

Emmaus

I've needed this journey
With its time
To walk along with you
To talk through the confusion
That clouded my dreams
To verbalise the fears
That have become
Less threatening
Now named

I've needed this time
To become more sensitive
To the fires
You ignite within
To grow beyond talking
Into communion.

New Life

In ground I thought was barren
Germinated a seed
A seed that lay dormant
For a long time
Waiting
For that someone
Who would call it to life
And create the climate
Where it had the courage
To surface
Above the ground
And be unafraid
To stand so vulnerable

That seed is still struggling
To allow its roots to grow deeper
Into the soil of God's love
And its shoot to stand strong
In its weakness
It struggles to understand
The contradiction
Of sun and rain

But for all its struggle
It touches mystery
And mystery is beauty
Born of God
Who is beyond all dreams
And understanding.

Journey into Life

Alone
In the cool of evening
High on the mountainside
Its breathtaking view
Somehow sensitised me
To Your presence
And to Your touch
Which dissolved barriers
Of anxiety
That closed up my world
Your love flooded
My being
Your glory
Bright and dazzling
Like a sudden burst
Of sunlight
Through a clouded sky

How I longed for time
To stand still
So that I could remain
Held by you
In the ecstasy of that moment
With nothing to disturb
Its tranquillity

But time moved on
And so did you

As you set out to descend
Into the valley below
And though reluctant to leave
That quiet place
I followed
Only knowing how much
I desired to be with you

And as I travel into
The valley of life
I know not where
You'll lead me
Or when the journey will end
But this I do know
That you are there
With and for me
And that someday I'll see
Things that today
Lie beyond my limited vision

May the fire lit within
On that mountainside
Never be quenched
Though at times
It may waver
In the storms of life.

White Lake

Standing on the hilltop
Overlooking the lake
Motionless with wonder
Captivated by the sheer beauty
And majesty of your creation
A beauty that
Quietened my mind
'Till scattered thoughts
Converged
To a still place
Deep inside
My heart beat
In unison
With the pulse of life
Once more aware
Of my creatureliness
And my need of you
My Creator.

Sand Candle

Behold a candle
A candle formed
In receptive sand
Womb of infinity
As many
Separate
Unique candles
Sharing their
Colour
Texture
Shape
Gave of their essence
To be poured out
In a new creation
With its intensified
Feminine hue
A widening experience
Deepening potential
To be set aflame
By a power
Beyond itself

Behold a candle
That yearns from the depths
Of its womanhood
To be a giver of light
Whose formation
Through irreversible blending
Has deepened its awareness

That the dangers
Of being blown out
Or burnt out
Can only be surmounted
Through core sharing

Behold a candle
That knows its need for space
For only when it is aflame
Can it be set aflame

A candle that needs
To be decisive
Unwavering
An integral part
Of the inspiration
That lights the way
Forward.

Skelligs

What held you here
In this remote place
Cut off from the mainland
What made you choose
Such close encounter
With loneliness and poverty

As my mind grappled
With these questions
My heart heard the answer
Whispered in the gentle breeze
In the stillness
Born of the beauty
Of this place
A place
God filled
Not God forsaken
Not cut off from life
But forcing one
To confront it.

Beyond the Horizon

I watched the ship
Sailing out to sea
Going further and further away
Until it disappeared from sight
Passing beyond the horizon

And as I watched
It brought you to my mind
And how I had seen you
Drift slowly away
Until you passed
Life's horizon
And were lost to my
Earthly sight

And as I stared out
At that now vacant space
I knew that ship
Though hidden from
My vision
Was still within that sea
And now
Nearer the place
It had set out to reach

And as I feel that empty space
Within

And your presence seems to be
Beyond my reach
I somehow know that you are near
Because you have reached
The eternal shore

A shore whose vastness
Knows no bounds
Whose limitlessness reaches
Beyond my limits
Whose fullness fills my emptiness
A shore which puts you beyond
My reach
But holds me within yours

And yet at times I do reach you
When I sail down the sea of
Time past
And there on the shore
Of memory
I taste the salt
Of the waves of love
And loneliness
That flow gently
O'er my heart.

Love

You are
To me
A bridge
To my deeper self
To the part of me
Where new dreams
Are born
Out of fragile possibilities
And old dreams
Rediscovered
Their essence
Undiminished
Though life's demands
Have brought them
To a seeming point
Of extinction.

Mountain Ascent

Often in my heart
I set out again
On that mountain ascent
Letting go of excess baggage
Non-essentials
For that journey
To the mountain top
That place of wider vision
Forcing confrontation
With life's essence
Its bracing wind
Sweeping through my being
'Till I am alert
To its inner path
And the life it calls forth
From within
The freshness of the air
I breathe
Filling me with a sense
Of being frail
Yet
God touched.

Dream's Tension

There is a growing tension
Within
Between dream and reality
For as the dream
That cries out
To be lived
Becomes clearer
So too
Do the chains
That imprison it.

Love's Touch

The depth of love
Tangible in your touch
Had no need of words
To proclaim itself
For words
Would only have sounded
Hollow
Amid the eloquence
Of silent communion.

Another Road

It wasn't easy
To admit defeat
To accept
That I had not the energy
To scale the heights
Others reached with ease
To be forced
To take a lonelier road
Away from the crowd
Into solitude
Yet there was freedom
In accepting limitations
The new road
Offering space
To come to terms
With where I had come from
And discover
Possibilities
For a new direction.

Setting Sail

Often I stood here
Watching as a ship set sail
For distant lands
Glad that it had parted me
From no one
Yet knowing
That someday
Someone I love
Would set sail
And be gone forever
From this shore

Yet nothing
Nothing
Prepared me
For the suddenness
Of your departure
No ship came
You were just swept up
Into the sea
Submerged forever

I wonder why
I return here
When assailed
By waves of anger
Anger at being robbed
Of those special

Presailing moments
With its time
For hugs and words of love

Yet I feel drawn here
To await the calm
That follows every storm
And the waves of healing
That flow from
Somewhere
Out there
And to experience
The sea's power
To amplify
And carry to me
From distant shore
Your whispered words
Of love.

Touch of Beauty

The beauty of this place
Gently speaks to me
Stirring within
A longing
To be here
Alone
To be touched
To the core
By its softness
Or
With someone
Who would not disturb
My communion
With its depths
Someone who could
Share its embrace
And understand
Its revelation.

Ghosts

The ghosts of time past
Haunt my night
Clamouring for attention
Their restlessness
Reinforced by the howling
Of the wind
Outside

Does my fear
Of the night
That signals their return
Disquiet them
Will trust empower them
To find peace
To become
Silent night shadows
That allow me
To drift into sleep
At last
Restful.

Stars

When night falls
And questions perplex
Stubbornness demanding answers
The twinkling stars appear
To gently tease
Reminding me
That though they lie
Within my vision
They too have secrets
As yet
Hidden
Revelation needing time.

Time

When ceaseless demands
Upon my time
Threaten to pull me apart
I seek a quiet shore
To listen to the gentle
Evenly spaced wavelets
That convey no urgency
Make no demands
And humanely mark time.

The River

What within
Colours our vision of you
There are some
Whose frayed senses
And inner conflict
Have resonated with
Your turbulent waters
And have lost
Their lives
In you

Others have sensed
The mysterious calm
Of your depths
Have been inspired
By the beauty
Of the sky touching you
With sunset colours
Finding life
And energy.

Gentle Strength

How fragile and vulnerable
You appear to be little flower
Standing alone amongst the rocks
Yet what inner strength
You must have
To have broken through
Barriers of coldness and hardness
Finding space in crevices
For your seed
To reach full potential.

Countryside

The sounds of distant
Bird and beast
Carried on the wind
Are barely audible
Not disturbing
The stillness I've found here
The stillness I've needed
To be recreated
By the tangible
Breath of the wind.

City Nights

My window is open wide
On a city
That looks so beautiful
It is quiet and peaceful
Now that night is here
With its easy rhythm
Into which I can relax

Yet another world
Exists out there
Darkness hiding life styles
In discord
With the music
Of the night.

Violets

Unassuming
Shy
You seem to shrink
From life
But those with vision
Know you lack
Neither life nor colour
And possess
A quiet power
That is challenging.

Where do I Live?

Where do I live?
Is my home
One built upon a hill
Its comfort
Cushioning me
From struggle
My image of God
Not disturbing
My complacency
Or do I live
Deep in the valley
In the midst of life's struggles
Its heart cry
For a God
With a human face
Echoing with my own.

Stained-Glass Windows

Morning comes
Chasing away the night
The sun's rays
Gently touching you
Transfiguring you
Dispelling the illusion
Of sameness
Created by the darkness

I feel within
A sense of wonder
At the beauty of
Your creation
The figures you depict
Now full of vitality
Their unique pattern
Of colours
Now visible

I long for a deepening
In me
Of God's love
A love that can dispel
The shadows that cloud
Who I really am
And penetrate the deepest recesses
Of my being
Making the uniqueness

Of my colour and texture
Speak
Of the transforming power
Of the Son.

Early Bloomer

You stand
Alone
Early bloomer
Conquering loneliness
In knowing solitude
Growing beyond
Self-centredness
Urging others
To surface
From the womb
Into spring.

Why?

Why God?
Why so much disfigurement
Of a world
Created to be beautiful?
Why so much fragmentation
Of lives
Born to be whole?

Why do we destroy
One another's dreams
In the restless pursuit
Of our own?

Why so much pain and suffering
When we are born to heal?
Why?
Why?
Why?
Endlessly questions my mind
While my heart
Seeks but to live the questions now
In the hope
That someday
I'll live into
your answers.

Following Stars

An unexpected star
Arose within
Lighting up the dark
Its awesome brightness
Compelling me to follow
As it journeyed
Along unfamiliar paths
Leading inwards
To Bethlehem
Beyond places
So overcrowded with possessions
There was no room left for Him
Beyond places
Too busy to have time
To encounter the stranger
That could become friend
Beyond places that wouldn't open
To the powerless
To a stable
Deep in the quiet
A stable
Poor but open
Vulnerable but real
Where He was born
And with Him
Truth
Beauty
Hope
And love beyond measure.

Feet of a Skater

Your music
Touches my core
Filling my being
With harmony
'Till inner feet
Long to skate
With graceful steps
Utterly responsive
To your rhythm

Yet outward steps
Are frozen hard
Like the ice
Beneath my feet
Frozen by fears
That hold back
The feet
Of the skater.

The Island

It is so still now
On this remote island
That I can hear
Whispered in the wind
The story of the sea
With nothing to
Interrupt it
But inner voices
That
Are soon silenced
In the face
Of refreshing simplicity.

The Seagull

How graceful you are
So attuned to the movement
Of the wind
To be one with it
As you soar upwards
In freedom
Yours is the gracefulness
I dream of
As I struggle
With my resistance
To the breath of the spirit
Within
Imprisoned in others' perception
Of me
Grounded by fear of being
Vulnerable

Yet like you
I hear the call
Of the sea
Feel the desire to be lost
In its solitude
Drawn to let go of
Who I am
And be emptied and transformed
In its changing tide
Allowing its power to
Cleanse me
And penetrate my humaness.

Crocuses

Decked in purple
Yellow
White
They dance beneath
Your leafless form
In joyful celebration
Of their spring

How you must smile within
At their brashness
As you stand
Unperturbed
By their jokes about
Your drabness
Or their questioning
Of what
To them appears
As your lack of life
The years of continual leafings
Each letting go
Have matured you
Mellowed you
And you know within
That while these dancers
Come and go
With each new tomorrow
You have stood the test of time
And in your graceful growing
Know eternal springs.

Soothing Power

Turbulence of thought
Calmed
By timeless constancy
Of waters' wash
Upon the sand
Frayed senses
Soothed
By its easy rhythm
Tight control
On emotions
Gently relaxed
In its embrace
Like a barnacle
Loosened
From tenacious grip

On rock.

Broken Shells

As I walked along
The sandy shore
I saw the tell tale signs
Of the night's storm
Broken shells
Tossed up from the
Sea's depths
Shells that would soon
Be washed away
Re-absorbed into the depths
Leaving no trace
Or scar upon the shore

And in that moment
I knew
That there is space
Within your vastness
For my brokenness
To surface
From the depths
Brokenness that will not
Destroy
If I too allow it
To be part
Of your ebb and flow.

Shore Wind

I was laden down
When I met you
With cares that seemed as many
As the pebbles on your shore
Afraid that letting go
Would mean losing control
And being blown
Into tiny pieces
By the strong wind
But the wind was gentle
With its strength
Not fragmenting
But unifying
Coursing through my being
'Till I felt whole
At one with myself
And with you
The sea.

The Sea

I found it hard
To leave the warmth
Of your embrace
And the feeling of completeness
Found
In love given freely

Yet we are not apart
For we are part
Of one another
And all it takes
Is a moment on an
Inner shore
To know again
The swell of your love.

Images

What is my image of God
Dare I share it?
Or am I afraid
That in doing so
I will reveal something
Of myself
To the other.

Is it a surface image
Easily tarnished
When exposed to life?
Or is it a reflection
Of a deeper truth
That challenges me
Urgently pushing me on
To embrace
My destiny.

Walls

What holds me
Within solid walls
When deep inside
I long to run
With the wind
Unbound
What use are walls
That offer security
If they also hide me
From myself
And keep out
Those I want to let in

What use are walls
If in keeping trouble out
They impound a spirit
Born to be free
And to dance with life.

The Other Shore

I feel within
A growing sense of calm
All anxieties conquered
By that dimly visible shore
Whose soothing waves
Calm
As they flow over
My tired body
Drawing me towards
The shore
That's getting clearer now
Into the peace
Of dwelling forever there
With and in you

Gone is the fear
Of being unprepared
You are near.

Silence

Silence
Rising up
From the heart
Of the bog
Its density
Pervading my being

I dared not speak
Lest words
Would break its hold
On me
And I longed
To grow into that silence
Like the blades of grass
Pushing up
From the earth
Allowing it
To greet
The silence
Becoming
In me.

Inner Journey

I have travelled afar
Walked the streets
Of London
Paris
Rome
Discovering new things
In exciting places

Yet nothing compares
To what I have seen
In the eyes of one
Who has never left
The confines
Of hospital ward
For more than forty years

Wisdom beckoned me
Through those eyes
A wisdom
Deeper than my knowledge
Born when impossibility
Of outer journeys
Forces inner ones
Leading to depths
Some of us
Only dream of reaching

And deep inside

I know
That while I have travelled
To distant places
He has travelled farther
On a journey
That has brought Him
To his centre
To know
Who he is
And who he can become
In God.

Words

What lessons have gone unlearned?
What dreams still sleep?
What gifts remain wrapped
Because I have not taken time
To retreat from the fast lane
Of this whirlwind existence
To listen to your words
Spoken in silence
Shaped in inner space.

Jim

You died in her arms
And in His
In a place
That had become home
Through the commitment
That had brought you there
Faithfully
Day by day
Despite rain
Hail
Snow

Your final journey
From that place
That was so much
A part of you
And you a part of it
Touched those of us
Who saw you go
And knew
We were witnessing
God's fidelity
Meeting yours.

Dulled Senses

Eyes forever turned inwards
Focused on past events
Are blind to the
Beauty of the present
Sunset colours
Reflected on the waters
Flowers dancing
In the wind
Sights that can tap
Hidden inner springs

Ears that are constantly
Tuned to inner fears
Fail to hear
The sounds of now
The barely audible rhythm
That can still
The core
Of one's being.

Awakening

Suddenly I felt again
The stirrings of new life
Within
Dreams awakening
Invigorating the awareness
Of the God
I once felt so deeply
His pulse strong
In the deepest recesses
Of my being
And the miracle of
That new burst of life
Took me by surprise
Like the coming of
Snowdrops in spring
Though awaited all winter
They come so silently
That the suddenness
Of their breaking
Through the hard earth
Takes your breath away

And the new life I felt within
Burst through with the words
You gave me space to say
Words that carried me
Unafraid
To the ground of my being
Where God

The source of that life
Was waiting
For me to allow Him
To love me.

Word Become Flesh

I watched you little bird
Flapping against the window pane
Struggling to be free
Trapped by inability to see
The open door
I longed for the language
To tell you
That there was a way
And stop you from hurting
Yourself
Needlessly

As that longing stirred within
I remembered my God
Whose love for his struggling people
Found a way to express itself
– In Word become flesh.

Desert Space

I stand on the edge
Of a new frontier
Challenged
To let go of the familiar
And journey into the wilderness
To confront the wild creatures
That lurk there
To pass through the desert space
Of solitude and loneliness
That will strip away
The false identities
Imposed by outside forces

Do I have the courage
To embrace this space
Or will I fill it with useless activity
To deaden its challenge
For before dream and reality
Merge within
Dream must question my reality
And reality
My dream.

Pheasant

Pheasant
Unrushed
Leading young
Across road
Halted my journey
Held me
Still
Reluctant to disturb
Such delicate
Balance
By the tiniest
Motion

Her unflustered pace
Forced me
To slow my own
My journey on
Less hurried
More deliberate.

The Deep

The quiet power
Of the calm sea
Flowed gently through my being
Calling me softly to become
One with it
On its journey
To that other shore
That's dimly outlined
Along the horizon
A shore that at times
I've caught a glimpse of
Or seen signs
That hint of the promise
It holds

Yet at times I stand
Rooted to this shore
Unable to take the plunge
Into the sea's depths
Bound by my fear of
Letting go
And being submerged in emptiness

Yet its vastness speaks of
Fullness
And only by being immersed
In its waters
Can I taste abundant life

And pass beyond surface pain
Into wholeness
I long for the courage
To launch out into the deep
With eyes upon Him
Who'll lead me to the other shore
The eternal land that's really
Not so far away
But already invades my being
When I live in the now.

Held by God

Rest a while
In the shelter of my arms
Safe from tempestuous winds
'Till my strength in you
Can withstand them

Feel my fingers
Gently touching you
In the breeze
'Till your tension subsides

Allow my Son
To dry away
Your tears
My rhythm
Lull.

Mirror Mirror

Mirror Mirror on the wall
'Who is the fairest of them all?'
Question
Seeking affirmation
Not truth
Making truth when spoken
Unacceptable
And she
Distorted by the anger
Welling up within
Became less fair
Through vengeance sought

Dare I look at my reflection
In the mirror of life
Eyes focused by the lens of truth
On a tarnished image.
Do I have the courage to accept
That I am not as fair
As I seek to be
To confront the pain
Of that truth
Growing through it
Beyond it
Until the blemishes fade
With light of acceptance
Reawakening dreams
To fairer be.

Vision

Like the microscope
With its power to make visible
The tiny world
Of micro-organisms
That would otherwise remain
Unseen
By human eye
And the telescope
That can bring into focus
The far away world
Of stars and planets
The inner eyes can behold
Things incapable of being seen
By human eyes alone
They can see the
Invisible realities
Of the eternal kingdom
That lie within
About
And beyond us
These eyes can see beyond the bread
To the body broken and shared for us
Can see beyond the wine
To the blood poured out
For love of us
Can see beyond pain and suffering
To life transformed in each
Letting go to Him

God
Touch my inner eyes
Heal their blindness
Teach me to look beyond
And perceive
What is truly real
So when my body's eyes
In death do close
My inner eyes will have already begun
To see you reflected
In all of life
And will be ready
For the total vision
As I meet you
Face to face.

Life Flow

Like a plug
Of clotted blood
Sealing off
Life flow
From heart
Unnamed fears
Undealt with anger
Block off
Energy flow
From centre
Leaving me
Less able
To live life
To full.

Yes

In precious moments
When the restlessness of my heart
Is stilled by the beauty of the sunset
Soothed by the harmony of a babbling brook
Caressed by the gentleness of your breath
Or touched by the softness of the rain
I am drawn into your quiet
There to behold a rainbow
Reminder of your covenant with me
Your promise to betroth yourself to me
                forever

Awed by the enormity of your faithfulness
Which is beyond words
A quiet YES is uttered somewhere in my
                depths

Yes to daring to say I am loved by you
So much
That you
My God, my creator
Are giving yourself to me forever

Yes to a love that will fulfil its promises in me
That will hold me
Through the darkness of my fears and doubts
When I can't see those promises coming true

And I have to learn to wait for you

Yes to wanting a heart
So sensitive to your touch
That my life becomes transparent
Radiating your love
A love that is deeper than my depths
Wider than my limits
More constant than my waverings

And so today I give you myself
As I know myself to be
And I give you who I may become
In allowing you to dream your dreams in me.

God's Touch

Into my inner turmoil
You came
Your gentle touch
Momentarily holding me
In timelessness
Suspended beyond fear
Wrapped in peace
And tranquillity

It was the touch
Of One
Yet Three
The touch of Father
Reaching out
Embracing me
Speaking His
Word of Love
Which became flesh
In the touch of the Son
It was the touch
Of the Spirit
Moving across
The inner fibres
Of my being
Stirring their response
To that Love
A love that left me
Saturated
With inexpressible
Joy and peace.

Yours Forever

Somewhere deep inside
I knew I was yours
As restlessly I sought
My destiny
Some thought I was a fool
To take the path I did
But I had to be true
To what was deepest in me
Giving you my life
To have and to hold
Forever

And you my God
Have guided me along my years
Through joy and sorrows
To unexpected places
That have held riches
Beyond measure
Infinitely more than I could
Have asked for
Or imagined

And as I face the unknown land
Of my future
I hold within the awareness
That while life may change
With the shifting sands
Of a new tomorrow

One thing remains constant
Your being there
With and for me
You have guided me through
My past
My future is yours.

The Island

Now that I have tasted
The richness
Of the island
I understand why
You return here
If at times
Inwardly
For on that island
Where mainland sounds
Recede
Only the deepest movements
Continue
And humanity is restored
By the non-human world.

The Candle-maker

Once upon a time there was a candle-maker who was renowned for the candles he created, not alone for their exquisite quality but also for the endless variety there existed among them. No two candles were quite alike in colour, shape or texture, each bore a distinct touch of the creator's hand.

The candles were valued by the people into whose lives they brought light. Each in her own way dispelled some corner of darkness in the days when there were no other means of doing so. They provided the light which facilitated works that might otherwise never have been completed. They knew what their role was. There was a definite need and they were able to meet this need, the need which had in fact called them into existence.

Years passed by and new forms of light appeared leaving the light of the candle in the shade. People soon neglected the candles, relegating them to cupboards and other out of the way places, their potential to be set aflame often going unrecognised in a world where uniqueness was sacrificed for efficiency.

The candles grew restless. Some felt isolated. Their role was no longer clear. Some felt moulded into a shape that no longer fired them or others, while deep in their centres they yearned to be givers of light.

The candle-maker saw their struggle. Knowing that the plans he had for them were ones of fulfilment and not wanting their potential to be snuffed out, he called them together to see if he could fan into a flame the spark of light he knew existed within them and among them.

Each candle had the chance to share her light, from those that were still aglow with enthusiasm to those that were experiencing burn out. Together they searched for the inspiration that would illuminate the way forward.

And as they shared and grew beyond the stage of trying to wax eloquent they journeyed to the core of their existence. Yes there were new efficient forms of light but there were also new pervasive forms of darkness that could only be overcome by a powerful light source. The candles had experienced that power within themselves, a power that could set them and the world alight, with the light that outshines all lights, but they felt the need for a new shape that would empower that light to shine brightly from within.

And so there exists in the candle-maker's house, a new mould for those candles that choose to be reshaped, a painful process that calls for a letting go of colour, shape and texture, to be poured out in a new creation. But the candle-maker has not lost his touch nor the element of surprise in all his creations.

Some candles today are making their way to the candle-maker's house, to refind their essence and be moulded into a new shape, a shape that will, for them, best enkindle the light within, allowing it to permeate today's darkness.

More Interesting Titles

Body-Mind Meditation
A Gateway to Spirituality

Louis Hughes, OP

You can take this book as your guide for a fascinating journey that need not take you beyond your own hall door. For it is an inward journey, and it will take you no further than God who, for those who want him as a friend, lives within. On the way to God-awareness, you will be invited to experience deep relaxation of body and mind.

Body-Mind Meditation can help you become a more integrated balanced person. It is an especially helpful approach to meditation if the pace of life is too fast for you, or if you find yourself frequently tense or exhausted.

SPIRITUALITY AND HOLISTIC LIVING

Sr. Theresa Feist

You are in search of wholeness. You have a body, mind and spiritual life. Your spirit cannot soar if your feet are heavy. Your mind is confused when your blood is stagnant. You need to care properly for your temple.

An Easy Guide to Meditation

Roy Eugene Davis

Meditation is the natural process to use to release tension, reduce stress, increase awareness, concentrate more effectively and be open to life. In this book you will learn how to meditate correctly for inner growth and spiritual awareness. Specific guidelines are provided to assist the beginner as well as the more advanced meditator. Here are proven techniques used by accomplished meditators for years: *prayer, mantra, sound–light contemplation, ways to expand consciousness and to experience transcendence.*

Benefits of correct meditation practice include: deep relaxation, stress reduction, inner calm, improved powers of intelligence, and strengthening of the immune system. People in all walks of life can find here the keys to living life as it was meant to be lived.

An Easy Guide to Meditation was written by one who knows how to meditate and who, for decades, has been teaching the process to thousands of people all over the world. Roy Eugene Davis has written many other books including *Our Awakening World, Secrets of Inner Power, With God We Can* and *God Has Given Us Every Good Thing.*

Over 100,000 copies sold.

PETER CALVAY HERMIT

Rayner Torkington

This is a fast moving and fascinating story of a young priest in search of holiness and of the hermit who helps him. The principles of Christian Spirituality are pinpointed with a ruthless accuracy that challenges the integrity of the reader, and dares him to abandon himself to the only One who can radically make him new. The author not only shows how prayer is the principal means of doing this, but he details a 'Blue Print' for prayer for the beginner, and outlines and explains the most ancient Christian prayer tradition, while maintaining the same compelling style throughout.

Over 34,000 copies of this bestseller have been sold.

PETER CALVAY PROPHET

Rayner Torkington

This book is first and foremost a brilliant exposition of the inner meaning of prayer and of the profound truths that underlie the spiritual life. Here at last is a voice that speaks with authority and consumate clarity amidst so much contemporary confusion, of the only One who makes all things new and of how to receive Him.

THE PURSUIT OF MEANING

Joseph Fabry

The Pursuit of Meaning is written for the millions of people who are healthy but believe they are sick, because they feel empty; for those who are looking for meaning in frantic activity, in money, power, excitement, sex, alcohol, drugs; for those who are looking for meaning in laws and rules and dogmas rather than searching for it personally. Every mature person has been expelled from his own paradise and lived through his own concentration camp. To help man endure this has always been the tasks of prophets, priests, philosophers and educators. Now they are joined by the psychologists. Logotherapy supplies one contemporary answer to man's age-old problem of how to live after the expulsion and how to find meaning during and after the trials of suffering.

TREASURY OF WOMEN SAINTS

RONDA DE SOLA CHERVIN

Here are the fascinating and inspiring stories of over two hundred women, including mothers, prophets, and interior women of the Spirit. From mothers like Elizabeth of Hungary and prophetic saints like Hildegarde of Bingen to mystics like Julian of Norwich, this treasury chronicles Catholicism's most beloved women saints from the early church to modern times.

Ideal for use in daily devotions, **TREASURY OF WOMEN SAINTS** includes two hundred entries. Each one provides a biographical sketch of one or more saints, a life application for the reader, and a prayer or meditation for the day.

YEAR OF GRACE
A Spiritual Journey

Andrew M. Greeley

Year of Grace, A Spiritual Journey is a record of one man's journey over a twelve month period, and the discoveries he made in that time.

Fr Greeley is the author of nineteen bestselling novels including *Cardinal Sins* and a biography, *Confessions of a Parish Priest*.

THE WAY OF A HEALER

Peter Gill

Introduction by Lilla Bek

THE WAY OF A HEALER deals with different aspects of healing, and the way that spiritual healing works in the lives of people. Healing means health, and health is wholeness. That word wholeness implies a number of separate parts coming together to make a complete whole. We are accustomed to the concept of body, mind and soul, and unless these different aspects of ourselves function together in harmony we have dis-harmony or dis-ease. If that condition of dis-ease is allowed to continue unchecked, ultimately we have disease or illness. Spiritual healing works at the physical, mental, emotional and spiritual levels of a person.

Today we stand upon the brink of the darkest age that could yet befall mankind, or, with a change of consciousness, upon the edge of a new and wonderful dawn to herald in a golden age. What that age will be depends upon what we make of it now. The immediate need is for a concept which will integrate us with the life of the solar system and, through the solar consciousness, link us with the life of the universe and the word of God. Our thinking must become much more expansive to embrace, not only humankind as we know it, but also the angel, elemental and nature kingdoms, and other realms not normally perceived by our physical sense.